"Come over to my house," said Fox to Chick.

"We will chat."

"You come over to MY house," said Chick to Fox.
"Then we will chat."

Chick went to her house.

Fox went too.

But then Chick said, "Come back at one."

So Fox came back at one.

But then Chick said, "Come back at three."

So Fox came back at three.

But then Chick said, "Come back at six."

How many more times will that Fox come back?

One time too many!